" London

# in Quotations

"

Compiled by
Jaqueline Mitchell

Bodleian Library
UNIVERSITY OF OXFORD

First published in 2014 by the
Bodleian Library
Broad Street
Oxford OX1 3BG
www.bodleianbookshop.co.uk

ISBN: 978 1 85124 401 0

Selection and arrangement © Bodleian Library
Cover design by Dot Little
Designed and typeset by Rod Teasdale in 11 on 13pt Jenson
Printed and bound by L.E.G.O. spa, Vicenza

British Library Catalogue in Publishing Data
A CIP record of this publication is available from
the British Library

I hope to see London once 'ere I die.

William Shakespeare
(1564–1616)

"

High Lords, deep Statesmen,
    Dutchesses, and Whores;
All ranks and stations, Publicans
    and Peers,
Grooms, Lawyers, Fiddlers, Bawds,
    and Auctioneers;
Prudes and Coquettes, the Ugly
    and the Fair,

The Pert, the Prim, the Dull, the
    Debonnair;
The Weak, the Strong, the Humble
    and the Proud,
All help'd to form the motley, mingled
    Crowd.

Count William Combe
(1741–1823)

London is the epitome of our times, and the Rome of to-day.

Ralph Waldo Emerson
(1803–1882)

London is a modern Babylon.

Benjamin Disraeli
(1804–1881)

Sir, when a man is tired of London, he is tired of life; for there is in London all that life can afford.

Samuel Johnson
(1709–1784)

A person who is tired of London is not necessarily tired of life; it might be that he just can't find a parking place, or is sick of being overcharged.

Paul Theroux
(b. 1941)

Much as I hate to agree with that
tedious old git Samuel Johnson …
I can't dispute it. After seven years
of living in the country in the sort of
place where a dead cow draws a crowd,
London can seem a bit dazzling.

Bill Bryson
(b. 1951)

The truth is, that in London it is always a sickly season. Nobody is healthy in London, nobody can be.

Jane Austen
(1775–1817)

A mighty mass of brick, and smoke, and
  shipping,
Dirty and dusty, but as wide as eye
Could reach, with here and there a sail
  just skipping
In sight, then lost amidst the forestry
Of masts; a wilderness of steeples
  peeping

On tiptoe through their sea-coal
   canopy;
A huge, dun cupola, like a foolscap
   crown
On a fool's head – and there is London
   Town.

Lord Byron
(1788–1824)

I had been in London innumerable times, and yet till that day I had never noticed one of the worst things about London – the fact that it costs money even to sit down.

George Orwell
(1903–1950)

Nothing is certain in London but expense.

William Shenstone
(1714–1763)

The greatest glory that has ever come to me was to be swallowed up in London, not knowing a soul, with no means of subsistence, and the fun of working till the stars went out.

J.M. Barrie
(1860–1937)

London is the largest of the bloated
modern cities; London is the smokiest;
London is the dirtiest; London is, if you
will, the most sombre; London is, if you
will, the most miserable. But London is
certainly the most amusing and the
most amused.

G.K. Chesterton
(1874–1936)

So large is the Extent of *London*, *Westminster* and *Southwark*, with their Suburbs and Liberties, that no Coachman nor Porter knows every Place in them.

William Stow
(n.d., published 1722)

Goodness me, but isn't London big? It seems to start about twenty minutes after you leave Dover and just goes on and on, mile after mile ...

Bill Bryson
(b. 1951)

Hell is a city much like London –
A populous and a smoky city;

Percy Bysshe Shelley
(1792–1822)

Forget six counties overhung with
    smoke,
Forget the snorting steam and piston
    stroke,
Forget the spreading of the hideous
    town;
Think rather of the pack-horse on the
    down,
And dream of London, small, and
    white, and clean.

William Morris
(1834–1896)

The Filth, Sir, of some Parts of the Town, and the Inequality and Ruggedness of others, cannot but in the Eyes of Foreigners disgrace our Nation, and incline them to imagine us a People, not only without Delicacy, but without Government.

George Carpenter,
Lord Tyrconnell
(1750–1805)

I behold London; a Human awful
wonder of God!

William Blake
(1757–1827)

It really is an insane city ... its intelligentsia is so hurried in the head that nothings stays there; its glamour smells of goat; there's no difference between good and bad.

Dylan Thomas
(1914–1953)

Sir, if you wish to have a just notion of the magnitude of this city, you must not be satisfied with seeing its great streets and squares, but must survey the innumerable little lanes and courts. It is not in the showy evolutions of buildings, but in the multiplicity of human habitations which are crowded together, that the wonderful immensity of London consists.

Samuel Johnson
(1709–1784)

... it is one of the largest Cities on Earth, yet it is governed with the same Ease, and with less Trouble to the Subject, than many petty Villages in other Parts of the World.

Robert Campbell
(n.d.)

“

London, that great sea, whose ebb
    and flow
At once is deaf and loud, and on the
    shore
Vomits its wrecks, and still howls on
    for more.
Yet in its depth what treasures!

Percy Bysshe Shelley
(1792–1822)

66

Like the majority of London people, she occupied a house of which the rent absurdly exceeded the due proportion of her income, a pleasant foible turned to such good account by London landlords.

George Gissing
(1857–1903)

> I have seen the West End, the parks, the fine squares; but I love the City far better. … The City is getting its living – the West End but enjoying its pleasure. At the West End you may be amused; but in the City you are deeply excited.

Charlotte Brontë
(1816–1855)

The lighted shops of the Strand and Fleet Street; the innumerable trades, tradesmen, and customers, coaches, waggons, playhouses; all the bustle and wickedness round about Covent Garden; the very women of the Town; the watchmen, drunken scenes, rattles; life awake, if you awake, at all hours of the night; ... I often shed tears in the motley Strand from fulness of joy at so much life.

Charles Lamb
(1775–1834)

Provided that the City of London remains as it is at present, the clearing-house of the world, any other nation may be its workshop.

Joseph Chamberlain
(1836–1914)

AH, London! London! our delight,
Great flower that opens but at night,
Great City of the midnight sun,
Whose day begins when day is done.

Richard Le Gallienne
(1866–1947)

London is the greatest show on earth, for never have so many human characters been gathered together at one place. Here, in a day, you can see the world.

Laurie Lee
(1914–1997)

London doesn't love the latent or the lurking ... It wants cash over the counter and letters ten feet high.

Henry James
(1843–1916)

[I]n the city of London, ... he had never, in the whole course of his life, found above three or four whom he could call thoroughly honest.

Tobias Smollett
(1721–1771)

I thought it was possible for a city clerk to be a gentleman.

George Grossmith
(1847–1912)

You must not expect much friendliness
from a John Bull who does not see
his way to get something out of you.
On the other hand, for learning
commerce, London is without exception
the best school.

Georgina Meinertzhagen
(1850–1914)

I do not at all like that city. ...
[W]hatever evil or malicious thing that
can be found in any part of the world,
you will find in that one city. ... if you
do not want to dwell with evildoers, do
not live in London.

Richard of Devizes
(*c*.1150–*c*.1200)

I don't know what London's coming
to – the higher the buildings the lower
the morals.

Noël Coward
(1899–1973)

'I love walking in London', said
Mrs Dalloway. 'Really, it's better
than walking in the country.'

Virginia Woolf
(1882–1941)

[T]he amusements of London seemed
as flat as soda-water that has been
standing in the sun.

John Buchan
(1875–1940)

... a duller spectacle this earth of ours
has not to show than a rainy Sunday
in London.

Thomas De Quincey
(1785–1859)

I landed in London on a wintry autumn evening. It was dark and raining, and I saw more fog and mud in a minute than I had seen in a year.

Charles Dickens
(1812–1870)

> LONDON, thou art of townes *A per se.*
> Soveraign of cities, seemliest in sight,
> Of high renoun, riches and royaltie;
> Of lordis, barons, and many a goodly
>   knyght;
> Of most delectable lusty ladies bright;
> Of famous prelatis, in habitis clericall;
> Of merchauntis full of substaunce
>   and of might;
> London, thou art the flour of Cities all.
>
> William Dunbar
> (1456?–1513?)

To a lover of books, the shops and
sales in London present irresistible
temptations.

Edward Gibbon
(1737–1794)

London is a riddle. Paris is an explanation.

G.K. Chesterton
(1874–1936)

How London doth pour out her citizens.

William Shakespeare
(1564–1616)

"

Sir, the spirits which I have in London
make me do every thing with more
readiness and vigour. I can talk twice as
much in London as any where else.

James Boswell
(1740–1795)

"

Gin ... is the principal Sustenance
(if it may be so called) of more than
an hundred thousand People in this
Metropolis.

Henry Fielding
(1707–1754)

London goes beyond any boundary or convention. It contains every wish or word ever spoken, every action or gesture ever made, every harsh or noble statement ever expressed. It is illimitable. It is Infinite London.

Peter Ackroyd
(b. 1949)

London; a nation, not a city.

Benjamin Disraeli
(1804–1881)

66

Then as to Bankruptcies, and other
Villanies of that Nature, the City of
London is so full of privileg'd Places,
where such Thieves may take Shelter,
that upon the whole it must be
Confess'd there is much less Danger in
being wicked at London than at Paris.

Henri Misson
(*c.*1650–1722)

"

So all that great foul city of London
there, … you fancy it is a city of work?
Not a street of it! It is a great city of
play; very nasty play and very hard play,
but still play.

John Ruskin
(1819–1900)

The Hours of the Day and Night are taken up in the Cities of London and Westminster by Peoples as different from each other as those who are born in different centuries.

Richard Steele
(1672–1729)

London crushes the imagination and tears the heart asunder.

Heinrich Heine
(1797–1856)

A man who can dominate a London
dinner-table can dominate the world.

Oscar Wilde
(1854–1900)

A man dressed to appear at Court would not dare to walk through the streets of London: a porter, a loafer, a scapegoat from the dregs of the people would throw mud at him, laugh in his face, push him to make him say something offensive, all in order to have an excuse for engaging him in a fist fight.

Casanova
(1725–1798)

London, that great cesspool into which all the loungers and idlers of the Empire are irresistibly drained.

Arthur Conan Doyle
(1859–1930)

The type of man capable of success
in London is more or less callous
and cynical. If I had the training of
boys, I would teach them to think of
London as the last place where life can
be lived worthily.

George Gissing
(1857–1903)

I like the spirit of this great London which I feel around me. Who but a coward would pass his whole life in hamlets; and for ever abandon his faculties to the eating rust of obscurity?

Charlotte Brontë
(1815–1856)

We can be nowhere private except in the midst of London.

Charles Lamb
(1775–1834)

66

London is a roost for every bird.

Benjamin Disraeli
(1804–1881)

With the possible exception of New York, there is no place like London for versatility in eating.

James Huneker
(1859–1921)

London is undoubtedly a place where
men and manners may be seen to the
best advantage.

James Boswell
(1740–1795)

The amount of women in London who flirt with their own husbands is perfectly scandalous. It looks so bad. It is simply washing one's clean linen in public.

Oscar Wilde
(1854–1900)

The Londoner seldom understands his city until it sweeps him, too, away from his moorings.

E.M. Forster
(1879–1970)

In a word, man in London is not quite
so good a creature as he is out of it.

John Galt
(1779–1839)

"

London streets ... are divided into two classes: into streets where the roast-beef of life is earned, and into streets where the said roast-beef is eaten.

Max Schlesinger
(1822–1881)

"

Would you know why I like London so much? Why if the world must consist of so many fools as it does, I choose to take them in the gross, and not made into separate pills, as they are prepared in the country.

Horace Walpole
(1717–1797)

I love London Society! I think it has immensely improved. It is entirely composed now of beautiful idiots and brilliant lunatics. Just what Society should be.

Oscar Wilde
(1854–1900)

In a town like London there are always
plenty of not quite certifiable lunatics
walking down the streets, and they tend
to gravitate towards bookshops, because
a bookshop is one of the few places
where you can hang about for a long
time without spending any money.

George Orwell
(1903–1950)

The sight of London to my exil'd eyes
Is as Elysium to a new-come soul;

Christopher Marlowe
(1564–1593)

The essential qualities of the city are closeness, variety, and intricacy, and the ever-recurring contrasts of tall and low, of large and small, of wide and narrow, of straight and crooked, the closes and retreats and odd leafy corners.

Sir Nikolaus Pevsner
(1902–1983)

Go where we may – rest where we will,
Eternal London haunts us still.

Thomas Moore
(1779–1852)

Houses, churches, mixed together,
Streets, unpleasant in all weather;
Prisons, palaces contiguous;
Gates, a bridge, the Thames irriguous.

[...]

Many a beau without a shilling;
Many a widow not unwilling;
Many a bargain, if you strike it:
This is London! How d'ye like it?

John Bancks
(1709–1751)

… the lowest and vilest alleys of London do not present a more dreadful record of sin than does the smiling and beautiful country-side.

Arthur Conan Doyle
(1859–1930)

The City is the Center of its Commerce and Wealth. The Court of its Gallantry and Splendor. The Out-parts of its Numbers and Mechanicks; and in all these, no City in the World can equal it.

Daniel Defoe
(1660–1731)

"

A town, such as London, where a man may wander for hours together without reaching the beginning of the end, without meeting the slightest hint which could lead to the inference that there is open country within reach, is a strange thing. This colossal centralisation, this heaping together of two and a half millions of human beings at one point, has multiplied the power of this two and a half millions a hundredfold; has raised London to the commercial capital of the world.

Frederick Engels
(1820–1895)

London, the Metropolis of Great-Britain, has been complained of, for Ages past, as a Kind of Monster, with a Head enormously large, and out of all Proportion to its Body.

Josiah Tucker
(1712–1799)

Of all quarters in the queer adventurous amalgam called London, Soho is perhaps least suited to the Forsyte spirit. ... Untidy, full of Greeks, Ishmaelites, cats, Italians, tomatoes, restaurants, organs, coloured stuffs, queer names, people looking out of upper windows, it dwells remote from the British Body Politic.

John Galsworthy
(1867–1933)

The two only inconveniences of London
are the excessive drinking of some
foolish people, and the frequent fires.

William Fitz-Stephen
(c.1180)

[We] saw the fire grow; and as it grow darker, appeared more and more, and in Corners and upon steeple and between churches and houses, as far as we could see up the hill of the City, in a most horrid malicious bloody flame ... It made me weep to see it.

Samuel Pepys
(1633–1703)

"

The tide of luxury has swept all the
inhabitants from the open country –
The poorest 'squire, as well as the richest
peer, must have his house in town …
The plough-boys, cow-herds, and lower
hinds … swarm up to London, in hopes
of getting into service, where they can
live luxuriously and wear fine clothes,
without being obliged to work.

Tobias Smollett
(1721–1771)

"

Soho ... with its muddy ways, and
slatternly passengers, and its lamps,
which had never been extinguished or
had been kindled afresh to combat this
mournful reinvasion of darkness,
seemed, in the lawyer's eyes, like a
district of some city in a nightmare.

Robert Louis Stevenson
(1850–1894)

> I long to go through the crowded streets of your mighty London, to be in the midst of the whirl and rush of humanity, to share its life, its change, its death, and all that makes it what it is.

Bram Stoker
(1847–1912)

London is a bad habit one hates to lose.

Anon.

Whenever a stranger is bold enough to hail a cab, not one, but half a dozen come at once, obedient to his call; and the eagerness the drivers display is truly touching.

Max Schlesinger
(1822–1881)

London's spiry turrets rise.
Think of its crimes, its cares, its pain.
Then shield me in the woods again.

James Thomson
(1914–1953)

# Credits

The publisher gratefully thanks the many copyright holders below who have generously granted permission for the use of the quotations in this book. Every effort has been made to credit copyright holders of the quotations used in this book. We apologize for any unintentional omissions or errors and will insert the appropriate acknowledgement to any companies or individuals in subsequent editions of the work.

p.1, William Shakespeare, *Henry IV Pt.II*, V.iii; pp.2–3, William Combe, *The First of April or The Triumphs of Folly* (1777), p.16; p.4, Ralph Waldo Emerson, *English Traits* (1856), ch.8 'Results'; p.5, Benjamin Disraeli, *Tancred* (1847), V.v.; p.6, Samuel Johnson, in ed. J. Bailey, *A Shorter Boswell* (1932), p.63; p.7, ©Paul Theroux, *Sunrise with Seamonsters* (1985), p.299; p.8, ©Bill Bryson, *Notes from a Small Island* (1995), p.56; p.9, Jane Austen, *Emma* (1815), ch.12; pp.10–11, Lord Byron (1819), *Don Juan*, X.82; p.12, George Orwell, *Down and Out in Paris and London* (1933), ch.29, by kind permission of the Estate of the late Sonia Brownell Orwell; p.13, *Works of William Shenstone*, III (1769), Ltr to Mr Graves, June 1742; p.14, J.M. Barrie, 'Courage' (Rectorial Address), 3 May 1922; p.15, G.K. Chesterton, 'Cockneys and their Jokes', *All Things Considered* (1915); p.16, William Stow, *Remarks on London* (1722), p.v; p.17, ©Bill Bryson, *Notes from a Small Island* (1995), p.41; p.18, Percy Bysshe Shelley, *Peter Bell the Third* (1839); p.19, William Morris, *Prologue: The Wanderers* (1868); p.20, George Carpenter Lord Tyrconnell, House of Commons Debate, Feb. 24, 1740–1; p.21, William Blake, *Jerusalem: The Emanation of the Great Albion* (1820); p.22, Dylan Thomas, Letter to Vernon Watkins (1983), ©The Trustees for the Copyright of Dylan Thomas; p.23, Samuel Johnson, in ed. J. Bailey, *A Shorter Boswell* (1932), p.167–8; p.24, Robert Campbell, *The London Tradesmen* (1847), p.303; p.25, Percy Bysshe Shelley, *A Letter to Maria Gisborne* (1820); p26, George Gissing, *New Grub Street* (1891), ch.18; p.27,

Charlotte Brontë, *Villette* (1853), ch.6; p.28, Charles Lamb, Letter to William Wordsworth, 30 Jan. 1801; p.29, Joseph Chamberlain, Speech Guildhall, London, 19 Jan. 1904; p.30, Richard Le Gallienne, *A Ballad of London* (1895), by kind permission of The Society of Authors as the Literary Representative of the Estate of Richard le Gallienne; p.31, ©Laurie Lee, *I Can't Stay Long* (1975), p. 45; p.32, Henry James, *The Awkward Age* (1899); pp.33, Tobias Smollett, *The Expedition of Humphrey Clinker* (1771), To Dr Lewis from Bramble, Bath, 19 May; p.34, George Grossmith, *The Diary of a Nobody* (1892), ch.1; p.35, Georgina Meinertzhagen, *A Bremen Family*, London (1912), p.251; p.36, *The Chronicle of Richard of Devizes of the Time of King Richard the First*, ed. J.T. Appleby (1963), pp.65–6; p.37, ©Noel Coward, *Collected Sketches and Lyrics* (1899-1973); p.38, Virginia Woolf, *Mrs Dalloway* (1925); p.40, Thomas de Quincy, *Confessions of an English Opium-Eater* (1821), 'The Pleasures of Opium'; p.41, Charles Dickens, *David Copperfield* (1850), ch.59; p.42, William Dunbar, 'In Honour of the City of London', *Oxford Book of English Verse*, ed. Quiller-Couch (1919), p.26; p.43, Edward Gibbon, *Memoirs of My Life* (1796), ed. J. Sheffield (1846), p.189; p.44, G.K. Chesterton (1915), 'An Essay on Two Cities', in *All Things Considered*; p.45, William Shakespeare (1564–1616), *Henry V*, IV.viii; p.46, James Boswell, *The Life of Samuel Johnson* (1913), vol.2, p. 170; p.47, Henry Fielding, *An Enquiry into the Causes of the Late Increase in Robbers* (1751) p.28; p.48, Peter Ackroyd, *London: The Biography* (2000), p.779; p.49, Benjamin Disraeli, p.50, Henri Misson, *Memoirs and Observations in his Travels over England* (1719), p.67; p.51, John Ruskin, *The Crown of Wild Olive*, Lecture 1: Work, sections 23–4 (1866); p.52, Richard Steele, *The Spectator*, 11 Aug. 1712; p.53, Heinrich Heine, in *Wolf Schneider, Babylon is Everywhere* (1960), p. 237; p.54, Oscar Wilde, *A Woman of No Importance* (1893), Act 3; p.55, Casanova, *History of My Life* (2006), p. 853; p.56, Arthur Conan Doyle, *A Study in Scarlet* (1887), Pt1, ch.1; p.57, George Gissing, *New Grub Street* (1891), ch.31; p.58, Charlotte Brontë, *Villette* (1853), ch.6; p. 59, Charles Lamb, Letter to William Wordsworth, 30 Jan 1801, *Complete Works*, vol.3, cited in *Selected English Letters* (1882); p.59, Mary Lamb, Letter to Thomas Manning, in *Mary Lamb* (1883), ch.4; p.60, Benjamin

Disraeli Lothair (1870), ch.11; p.61, James Huneker, *New York Times*, 27 Sept., 1914; p.62, *Boswell's London Journal*, 1762–63, ed. Pottle (2004), p.268; p.63, Oscar Wilde, *The Importance of Being Earnest* (1895), Act 1; p.64, E.M. Forster, *Howard's End* (1910), ch.13; p.65, John Galt, *The Ayrshire Legatees* (1895), ch.7; p.66, Max Schlesinger, *Saunterings in and about London* (1853), p.13; p.67, *The Letters of Horace Walpole, Earl of Orford*, vol.1, 1735–1748, Letter to Sir Horace Mann, 3 Oct., 174; p.68, Oscar Wilde, *An Ideal Husband* (1895), Act 1; p.69, George Orwell, 'Bookshop Memories' (1936); p.70, Christopher Marlowe, *Edward the Second* (1594), I.i; p.71, Nikolaus Pevsner, The Buildings of England, London vol.1, *The Cities of London and Westminster* (1973) pp.109–10; p.72, Thomas Moore, in *Rhymes on the Road, Fables, etc.*, by Thomas Brown the younger, (1823), p.27; p.73, John Bancks, 'A Description of London' (1738), p.27; p.74, Arthur Conan Doyle, *The Copper Beeches* (1892); p.75, Daniel Defoe, *A tour thro' the whole island of Great Britain, divided into circuits or journies* (1927); p.77, Frederick Engels, *Condition of the Working Class in England* (1845); p.78, Josiah Tucker, *Four Letters on Important National Subjects* (1783) Ltr II; p.79, John Galsworthy, *The Forsyte Saga* (1922), vol.II, In Chancery, p. 372; p.80, William Fitz-Stephen, *Fitz-Stephen's Description of the City of London* (1772), pp. 42–3; p.81, *The Diary of Samuel Pepys*, 2 Sept.1666; p.82, p.39, Tobias Smollett, *The Expedition of Humphrey Clinker* (1771), *To Dr Lewis from Bramble, Bath*, 19 May; p.83, Robert Louis Stevenson, *The Strange Case of Dr Jekyll and Mr Hyde* (1886), The Carew Murder Case; p.84, Bram Stoker, *Dracula* (1897), ch.2; p.86, Max Schlesinger, *Saunterings in and about London* (1853), p.158; p.87, James Thomson, 'Hymn on Solitude' in *Poems*, ed. Bayne (1900).